Talks About Old Nantucket

CHRISTOPHER COFFIN HUSSEY

Talks About Old Nantucket

By
Christopher Coffin Hussey

PREFACE

It is much to be regretted that, owing to the author's feeble state of health while writing this little book, more time and care could not have been given it.

It was left in an unfinished state. It has, however, been a great pleasure to do the little work which was necessary before giving the manuscript to the lovers of old Nantucket, for whom it was especially written.

LYDIA COFFIN HUSSEY.

FEW places in our country have acquired so much interest, and that of an unusual and quaint nature, as the island of Nantucket. Peculiar in its isolated situation and in the nature of its business, from which for nearly two hundred years its inhabitants derived their support; peculiar in its religious faith—that of the Society of Friends—which obtained in its history such preponderance as to become a sort of national religion, and to mould and color the entire life of the island—peculiar in becoming the third town in commercial importance in the Commonwealth, and then declining to the entire loss of its shipping, and the lessening of its population to one-third of the number in its prosperous days; peculiar from these combined causes, the island has gathered about itself a unique and singular fascination to all connected with it by their ancestry or by their own residence there, as well as to the large number from all parts of the country who have made it their summer home of latter years.

Born on the island (my ancestry dating back to its first settlement), with a natural taste for the old and quaint, I picked up without knowing it, and without purpose of its use or preservation, a considerable store of island lore, tradition, legend and story, which frequently formed subjects of conversation in leisure hours. Being often urged to put this into some form for preservation, I at length yielded to the solicitations, out of regard chiefly to my dear family and to my many valued friends, to whom I dedicate this little book, calling it, for want of a better name, "Talks About Old Nantucket."

Talks About Old Nantucket

Chapter I

ANTUCKET, that quaint old town on the sea, a spot dearer to its children than any other place on earth, is in its decadence, still clothed with a fascination of interest such as few places ever possess even to the stranger. It is a low, level, sandy island, once wooded, although never heavily, and now for the last century nearly destitute of a tree of original growth; fertile only in occasional spots, and destitute of the picturesque except for the grand surroundings of ocean.

How it ever came to be settled and, greater wonder, how its population ever rose to nearly ten thousand, are questions which have often been asked. A partial answer is doubtless found in its location, and another solution may be found in the strong love of home and aversion to change of residence inherent in those born and reared on an island.

Some years ago I was at Bedford Pool, Me., where I found several families by the name of Hussey. I discovered in an old cemetery so many of the name, beside those of other Nantucket families, that I became convinced there must have been at an eailier time some close connection between the places. On inquiry I could learn nothing. I wrote to my esteemed cousin, Eliza Barney, of Nantucket, the genealogist, who gave me a bit of romance. It seems that about the middle of the last century, two brothers, Bachellor and Christopher Hussey, prominent members of the Society of Fiiends, had a misunderstanding about landed property. Not being able to live in unity, and retain their membership in the meeting where the query was asked monthly, "Are love and unity maintained amongst you?" one of them took his family of nine childien and went down to what was then called Fletcher's Neck, now called Biddeford Pool, and settled there, afterwards diawing from Nantucket a few families. In going they left much and went to little, and soon the children becoming men and women drifted to their old home and were the ancestors of prominent families in New Bedford and Nantucket. As I looked on the location they chose at the Pool, it was interesting to see that, like our English ancestors, in settling in America they carried the home instinct with them, and chose spots near the haibor and shore and creeks, very like the Hussey homes on the island.

Tradition tells of a visit to the island of the Northmen at some unknown eaily period, as well as of their visits to other points along the Atlantic coast. As far as Nantucket is concerned, this is mere tradition, with nothing to verify it. The authenticated history of the island begins with its discovery in 1602 by Bartholomew Gosnold, an Englishman. He sailed from England in a small bark with thirty-two persons, bound for Virginia in search of a proper seat for a plantation. Having fallen in with

8

the Cape Shore (Cape Cod) late in the day, to avoid danger he stood off to sea, and in the night came in sight of the white cliffs at the east end of Nantucket, now Sankaty Head, the highest land on that part of the island. Whence arose the name of the island we are uncertain. There have been fanciful traditions concerning it, but it is generally thought that Nautican, known by ancient voyagers, and Nantucket are the same. We find no other record concerning Nantucket until the year 1641, at which time the whole island was deeded to Thomas Mayhew and his son Thomas, by James Faurett, agent to William, Earl of Sterling. The first emigration of the whites to the island forms one of the most interesting points in its history.

Thomas Macy was the first settler. In the year 1640, being then a young man, he moved with his family from the town of Chilmark, in Wiltshire, England, and settled in Salisbury, County of Essex, in Massachusetts. He lived here in good repute twenty years, where he acquired a good interest, consisting of a tract of land of one thousand acres, a good house and considerable stock. When this part of the country became more thickly settled by the English, dissensions arose among the people in regard to religion. Among other restraining laws, one was made that any person who should entertain one of the people called Quakers should pay a fine of five pounds for every hour during which he so entertained him. Thomas Macy subjected himself to the rigor of this law by giving shelter to a Quaker preacher who stopped at his house in a storm. This act was soon sounded abroad, for, being actuated by a sense of duty, he had used no means to conceal it. When cited to answer for the offence he addressed a letter to the court, the original of which is preserved in the cabinet of the Nantucket Athenæum, where it can be read by all who are interested. He could now no longer live in peace and in the enjoyment of religious freedom among his own people, and he chose to remove his family to a place unsettled by the whites, to take up his abode among savages where he could safely imitate the example of Jesus Christ, and where religious zeal had not yet discovered a crime in hospitality, or the refinements of civil law a punishment for its practice.

In the autumn of 1659, he embarked in an open boat with his family and such effects as he could conveniently take with him, and, with the assistance of Edward Starbuck, proceeded along the shore until they were abreast of the island; thence they crossed Vineyard Sound and landed on Nantucket. Their first care was to establish a good understanding with the natives, whom they found very numerous, and who flocked around them in amazement, having never before had an opportunity to see English people on the island. The natives were kind and hospitable, and readily lent their aid whenever they could make themselves useful. It being now late in the autumn, the care was to build a shelter for the family. There they spent the winter, the only white family, confined on the island among Indians, of whose character and language they were almost entirely ignorant. In the spring following, Edward Starbuck returned to Salisbury, where he was met with rejoicing by his friends, who had felt doubtful of his safe return. The same year he returned to the island, accompanied by eight or ten families.

Chapter II

HERE is little recorded of the life of the Islanders. A unique life it was, of simple habits, the people being closely allied by family ties and by a similarity of pursuits and interests. Their support was derived from the sea and such farming as the soil of the island allowed. At that early stage of the country's growth, the whales which sought the shallow waters of the coast near Nantucket were taken with comparative ease for they were then undisturbed by the commerce of the ocean, which later drove them to remote regions. The Islanders soon began to pursue and capture them in open boats, putting off from the shore and returning at night. Many of the Indians joining in this business became as expert whalemen as the white men. These beginnings of the whaling business with simple, crude methods have much of quaint interest, which those cannot realize who knew the business only in later years, when the ships of Nantucket were seen in every sea and the voyages were three or four years in length.

At the south of the site of the present town was a range of hills, called later Mill Hills, from the wind mills there, only one of which remains*. On the highest of these hills a spar was erected with cleats across it, not unlike a vessel's shroud, as a lookout for whales near the shore. When the signal was given "There she blows!" and the direction announced, the boats would put off in pursuit; the whales were tried out in small try-houses

*Now owned by the Historical Society of Nantucket.

built at convenient places along the coast. An old citizen, standing one day on Mill Hills and looking off over the ocean, said, "There is the pasture where our children's children will go for bread." So it proved. It was the pasture whence came in after years the support and wealth of as prosperous and happy a community as the country or the world ever had, until by the increase of maritime commerce the whales were driven to more distant regions, making whaling more hazardous; and the discovery of other means of lighting rendering less remunerative, it gradually declined and finally ceased on the island. The ships, one by one, were hauled up and either sold abroad or were abandoned. All the numerous factories were gradually taken down; the wharves once full of busy life, where fortunes from the sea were landed and again shipped to many parts of the world, were deserted and fell into decay, grass grew in the streets, and silence unbroken and oppressive settled over the former dwelling place of prosperous, contented industry.

Previous to the close of the seventeenth century, the records of the island are meagre, reminding one of the "short and simple annals of the poor," and not much of oral tradition of that period was handed down.

In the next half century the increase of the whaling business and of the population brought many marked changes. The most conspicuous of these was the change in the site of the town. The harbor at the west end of the island, called Maddequet Harbor, was found to be too small, while it was not sufficiently land-locked to be protected from northerly and easterly gales, and the harbor which is now used, being larger and much better adapted in every way to the wants of the island, gradually supplanted the other. Previous to this change the most thickly settled part of the island was in the region along the north shore, within a radius of about a mile east, south and west of the present reservoir of water-works. I used to hear in my boyhood an acquaintance, who was then in advanced life, say that his father remembered when the lane about a mile from the western end of the present Main street and a little east of the lot marked as the site of the house where Dr. Franklin's mother was born, was thickly enough settled to be called a street. There has not been a dwelling house on it for a hundred years, except a small one built in comparatively late years for a summer residence. Another aged friend said he remembered when meeting was done at the Friends' meeting house, which stood from 1736 to 1790 at the present Friends' burying ground at the west end of Main street, more people went west than east to go to their homes. One looking at the present situation finds it difficult to realize this.

The soil in the western part of the island was not sufficiently fertile to sustain a farming population, and when the harbor was changed many houses were removed to the locality of the new town. Several of these are still standing and retain their identity.

At this date but one house of the original town is left standing where it was built, in 1725, by Elihu Coleman, a noted preacher in the Society of Friends, who was born in 1700 and died in 1789. The house must have been exceedingly well built, as it is still in a good state of preservation, remarkably level

13

and upright for one so old. That it may be preserved as a monument of a noble past, through the sentiment of either some of the descendants of Elihu Coleman or of the island people themselves, is much to be desired.

Standing there in imposing proportions and appearance, as seen across the plains, alone left of all the settlement of which it was once a part, something sublime gathers around it. Its stately form is the same, the arrangements of the interior have scarcely been changed, the big kitchen fireplace with oven in the back remains as it was. To the lover of antiquity the whole house is very satisfactory, and its appearance shows that the owner as a house builder, as well as a minister, was ahead of his times, though without much book lore. What is said to have held Friend Coleman's library can still be seen—a shelf over the door of the west front room leading to the kitchen. In the exceeding smallness of its capacity there was no room for speculative theology or mere theories of religion, but it may be better adapted to draw from the deep foundations than the costly libraries of many modern ministers' studies laden with scholastic erudition.

In the southwest corner of this room I saw standing, in 1840, the clock for which they sent to England the year in which the house was built. A granddaughter of the family herself, then old, said to me, "My Grandfather sent to England forty pounds of whalebone, which a little more than paid for the clock, and for change there was returned a copy of Sewall's History." The clock had never been known to stop, except from neglect in winding, but once, and that was from the shock of the great Lisbon earthquake in 1755, which shock was felt throughout New England.

OLD COFFIN HOUSE, BUILT 1686

The oldest house now standing in the town proper, built in 1685, is the one at the North Shore, as it used to be called, belonging originally to the Coffin family, and within a few years has been put in condition for preservation by Tristram Coffin, Esq., of Poughkeepsie, New York. Connected with its history is a tradition of some interest. The owner of the house went from home very early one morning to go fishing, leaving his wife and young child sleeping in a room on the lower floor. Suddenly there appeared an Indian, who is supposed to have entered and gone up stairs, where he fell through the imperfect floor into a closet which opened into the room where the woman was. He went to the hearth, sharpened his knife, then blew out the light. The brave woman made no outcry, but seizing the child sprang past the Indian, who was intoxicated, and running to her father's house, which was not far distant, gave the alarm which caused the Indian to be secured.

The oldest house on the island, at the present time very much in ruins, is that known as the George Swain house, at Polpis, built in 1673. It is a low, small house, and has no especial history. There has always been something of strange, pathetic interest to the writer, in standing in front of this forsaken home, which, like all early houses, faces the south and looks off towards the southeast quarter. There is an indescribable impression in the silent landscape, and if two houses, one near the other remote, could be taken away and a few wigwams scattered around, it would be much as it was when the original inhabitants first looked out over the wide expanse of moor and swamps, with a patch of woods visible here and there, and wondered if a southeast storm were gathering, as the clouds hove up over "Tom Never's Head."

Another house at Polpis, not now standing, was built two years after the George Swain house, on what was known as the Hannah Meader Farm, later the Prince Gardner Farm. This was a larger house, used for many years by Hannah Meader as a house of entertainment for people riding out from town, and has something of a history. Not far from the back of the house ran a small stream, in olden time. Across this stream stood a small English-built house, in which died one of the last of the Indians who were carried off by the great Indian sickness. A daughter of Hannah Meader, who lived to be nearly one hundred, told me in my boyhood that she remembered going with her mother to the edge of the stream, still traceable, to carry food to the stricken Indians. For fear of taking the sickness she would put her pail by the stream, shout to the indians, and then leave. This small house was moved to town, enlarged, and was standing on York street, a little way out of Orange street, until within a few years. This aged woman told also of an intoxicated Indian who came to her mother's in the evening in the absence of her father, and clamored at the back door for admittance. She was a small girl, and a little child lay asleep in the cradle. The mother took from the "mantle tree shelf," as it was then called, a tortoise shell snuff box, and told her she would give it to her if she would sit still, make no noise, and rock the cradle till she returned. Thinking the Indian would not venture around to the front door, she went out that way and ran to the nearest neighbor, not less than

16

half a mile, where she obtained two men who returned with her, and found the intruder still at his post. "Let me open the door," she said, which she did, and before the Indian was secured he made a wound on that brave woman's neck, the scar of which remained to her death.

The frames of two houses of special historic interest, removed from the old to the new town, are still standing, and probably but little known. One is the north part of the house on Pine street, once owned by John Folger. This was the house of Nathaniel Starbuck and Mary, his wife, the "Great Woman," as she was called. It was often spoken of as the "Parliament House," from the fact that the town meetings were held there. The other is the house on Milk street, next west of the house on the corner of "New Dollar Lane." This was the house of Nathaniel Starbuck, Jr., son of Nathaniel and Mary. He was one of the preachers, and the first clerk of Friends' Meeting. Many houses of special interest, and other buildings connected with the early history of the town, were destroyed in the great fire of 1846. The loss of these was other than pecuniarily very great. To be able to go about in the lower part of the town among its prominent buildings and quaint streets and lanes, as they were in the olden time and in the prosperous days of the island, would be an inexhaustible mine of interest to the great numbers of visitors to the island of later years, especially to those who once lived there, to whom old associations are very dear.

The sites of the William Rotch house and store, the Samuel Rodman, and the Hammet house, which stood where now the Pacific Bank stands, and many others are still known and possess an interest attached to all buildings in which has flowed the life of the homes of those long since passed away.

A house of some historic interest is the one on Orange street, on the west side, a little above the railroad crossing, remodelled by Allen Smith. It was built by Abigail Howes, daughter of Steven Hussey, the founder of the Hussey family on Nantucket, whose estate was "across the Creeks." The house was built in 1704, and was considered at the time a great piece of extravagance. The bricks came from Holland, the windows were one pane of glass wider than the regulation width of the period ; the front stairs had balusters which ran quite to the garret. The carpenters came from Boston and boarded in an ancient house opposite, which has been gone but a few years. The remark was often made " Abigail Howes must be crazy to be building such a house. " The Husseys as a race were inclined to be progressive and a little fond of style. It may be it was a family trait developed by a short residence in Boston in her husband's day that accounts for the wider windows, the stair railing, and the absence of the long slope back roof. A touching incident of the husband's death is preserved. He and his young wife went to visit his friends on the main land in an open boat, accompanied by an Indian. When returning, in crossing the bar, the husband, who had the steering oar, slipped and fell overboard. The Indian was too much frightened to save him, and the wife, seizing the oar, managed to get near her father's house, when she gave out and fell fainting on the beach. For her son, born after her husband's death, she built the house on Orange street.

The William Macy house, which stood on the corner of Main and Federal streets, attracted the attention of hundreds when it was taken down by its large chimneys, which had in the lower story alone four of the old-time square jamb fire-places, of not less than nine or ten feet each in width. The necessary contraction in the width of the chimney before it came out of the roof was so great that one tier of bricks fell so much back of the one below it as to furnish steps up which one fearless boy walked to the top after the house had been taken away. A good story is told of one who occupied the house after the lower part was converted into stores. He thought the house was on fire, but could not discover its source so went to bed, to find in the morning, when the store was opened, coals dropping on the counter. The trimmer, the timber which supported the chamber hearth, was so large that it smouldered all night and had only just worked through. It was humorously told that the mason who took down the chimney offered to the owner to build him a brick house and take the bricks left as pay for his work.

The Samson house, afterwards the Daniel Jones house, on Orange street, probably the first with brick ends, was built about 1790. It was a fine house then, and is so still, with its front changed from wood to brick about fifty years ago. Nearly opposite this house, a little back of those now forming the east side of Orange street, north of and near what is now Stone Alley, stood an unpretentious house, around which two or three interesting incidents gathered. The house, like some others of early times, was framed on the main land. When it was being erected it was found to be upright all around, the two back stories high like the front, and so without the regulation long back roof.

To some of the Islanders this caused uneasiness, as being likely to introduce change and extravagance. A citizens' meeting was convened and the owner requested to cut down the back posts. Good man as he was he complied, which, it was humorously told, made the back door so low as to occasion the bumping of his head the rest of his life.

At one time a fishing vessel fell in with a wreck which proved something of a prize. The crew on their return were not equal to reckoning each one's share of the prize money. Debating what to do, one said, "There is Ruth Gardner, whose husband was the owner of this house, her father was a schoolmaster, and I guess she can reckon it." They went to her and told her the circumstances. She took the large bellows hanging by the side of the fireplace, took a piece of chalk from her pocket, and quickly told what each one's share was.

A daughter of the family, whom I remember in her old age as a person of much excellence of character, and a valued elder among Friends, told me her mother said to her when she was a young woman, "Eunice, why does not thee open a school? Thee knows the verbs and the articles, and I will come once a week and do the whipping."

An excuse of Ruth Gardner, widow of Nathaniel, for not attending a wedding to which she was invited on the day she entered her ninety-third year, is written in verse.

> King David, Barzillar did invite
> To make his home at court;
> His favors he did never slight,
> But to him did report.

This day thy servant is fourscore ;
    No beauties can she see,
Or music can she hear no more,
    In dainties tasted free.

Let this be my excuse ;
    To that I add twelve years.
My organs are all out of use,
    Though thy favors I revere.

Altho' I am thy only aunt.
    Yet thou must me excuse,
For to attend I surely can't
    Or be of any use.

This by the daughter Eunice, written in her eighty-third year, is of equal interest :

[*To the four boys who raised the largest edifice of snow before the back windows of our house that I ever saw.*]

No magic e'er raised this pile,
    Enchantment had no power,
But youthful energy and skill
    Toiled for it many an hour.

There is a charm to work on things
    That no resistance shows ;
With plastic hands you gave the shape
    And built a house of snow.

A mistress of the fur-clad Russ
    Once followed the device,
To raise a palace bright and clear
    Composed of naught but ice.

How long it stood they did not tell,
　But this we all may know,—
That, evanescent as it was,
　It passed away like snow

May you, dear boys, when youth has passed,
　And manhood bears its sway,
A trophy raise of virtuous deeds,
　That ne'er can melt away!

A pathetic incident is also connected with the house. In the time of the sickness which carried off the Indians, one called with whom there had been some barter. He said, "I want to settle with you, Mrs. Gardner, for I shall not live long." She tried in vain to dissuade him from this feeling. "I see it," he said, "under my finger nails. I feel it all over. The Great Spirit has shown it to me." The business was settled with much kindness and he started for his home at Squam Head, about nine miles away, at the east end of the island, but did not reach there, his prediction being fulfilled at a wigwam on the way.

There moved into this neighborhood, in the time of the Revolution, a family of wealth from Boston, going to the island for greater security. One day, one of the family went to neighbor Gardner's and asked if he might bring in and hide in their house a bag of specie, thinking as they were Quakers it would be safer there. The mother said, "Yes, but we must know nothing about it. Wait until we are all gone to meeting, then come in and put it where thee sees fit." It was hidden in a nook of the chimney. Some time after, a son of the family was bounding a ball, when it went up the chimney and lodged. In trying to recover it the bag was knocked down, and the owner was sent for to find another hiding place. It was a son of this house who brought to the island, from France, its first umbrella. From the same feeling that led the father to cut down the back posts of the house it was left unused. My old friend who kept the school was going with some of her young companions to ride to Sconset. She asked her mother if she might take the umbrella as a protection from the sun. "Yes," she said, "with the promise that thee will not open it until thee gets out of the town, and have it closed and put in the bottom of the cart when thee returns."

Speaking of the first umbrella reminds me of my mother's telling of the first chaise on the island. I remember the small building in which it was kept, of which there were many about the town in my boyhood, called chaise-houses. There was, my mother said, so general a feeling that a "shay" was too luxurious for common use that the first one was only used when lent for a funeral or for the use of an invalid.

A house in the northern part of the town, known as the Charles Gardner house, stands, off from any street, on a little elevation that used to be called "Gull Island," which in early time was nearly surrounded by water at some seasons of the year. This house in its changed form is still a stately mansion. I heard Captain Gardner, one of the owners of the house, a courtly Quaker gentleman, relate some incidents of his boyhood. Two members of the family, with some other Nantucket men, went to the main land for the purpose of procuring wood and timber. They took their provisions with them and made arrangements

with a woman of the place to cook their meals. They showed
her a bag of coffee unburned, with the request that they might
have some for dinner. When they sat down to the table at
noon, their hostess seemed anxious and told them she had put on
the coffee to boil as soon as they left, with a good piece of salt
pork, but it was as hard as ever and she was afraid they would
not be able to eat it. In the fall a piece of cloth was sent to the
main land to be filled, preparatory to being made into an overcoat for one of the family. It being the time of the Revolutionary War, the vessel was captured by an English privateer, and
the boy lost his coat. However, Charles must have a coat.
There was wool in the house, both black and white, and hearts
and hands willing to work. The mothers and sisters soon spun
and wove another piece of cloth; but not willing to risk trans-
portation again, it was put into a pounding barrel outside the back
door, and the rule made that each member of the family, when
he or she passed in or out, should pound a certain number of times
until the cloth was sufficiently filled. The wearer lived to acquire
a handsome property, was one of our most respected ship captains, and lived to wear much finer cloth, but he said, "I never
had a warmer or better coat." It may be he was not so devoid
of sentiment but that a mother's and sisters' love enhanced the
value of the coat, for he was a man of fine sensibilities.

KEZIAH FANNING
Daughter of Keziah Coffin (Miriam Coffin), heroine of the
novel called "Miriam Coffin," or "The Whale Fisherman."

Chapter III

ET us talk now of some of the Nantucket people. Our sea-coast towns abound in characters of local notoriety and incidents grave or humorous connected with them. Nantucket has had abundance of these. . From the fact that the men of the island were so generally at sea, the women enter largely into this list, as they did into the entire life of the town. It was they who chiefly had the rearing of the children and the management of the family's finances. They were for a long period the main teachers of the town, and from the nature of Friends' principles as to the ministry they were often also the ministers.

In my boyhood I was one day accosted by a stranger, who asked me if the large house on the corner of Main and Pleasant streets was the Friends' meeting house. I told him it was. He said, "Elihu Coleman was one of my ancestors and preached in that house. I wonder if I could get a shingle to take with me, and have something made as a souvenir?" I said, "I think so, as the building is soon to be taken down." I took him around to the south side, where I thought there were some of the original ones, which had survived the moving of the house nearly fifty years before. He found one, much guttered and worn, which he prized highly. It seems he was on the island gathering material for his book, "Miriam Coffin." He introduced himself to Franklin Folger, of Sconset, as Mr. Thompson, desiring to preserve his incognito, but afterwards proved to be a Mr. Hart, of New York. I have often wished I knew into what that large, weather-beaten, cedar shingle was wrought by our friend, and whether prized and preserved by any of his descendants. I have often wished that I had been then as familiar with the family as I have been since, and could have told him anecdotes of them and their place of residence.

The real name of the heroine of the book, "Miriam Coffin," was Keziah Coffin. She was one of the remarkable women of the island, and had she lived in a manner more in keeping with the Islander's sense of a sturdy, noble character, would have been enrolled among the distinguished women of Massachusetts of the last century. The book, by the way, I would commend to you as giving as good a representation of the life of earlier settlers of the island as can be found, for it is in the main a true description as well as an interesting one. I had the advantage, when reading the book, of knowing a woman (nearly a hundred years old), whose memory was still good, and conversing much with her about the different scenes and persons the book mentions. The incidents of the book have for the most part a basis of reality, although put together with a novelist's license. My old friend told me the real names of the persons mentioned and also the names of the localities, all of which I visited.

Miriam Coffin's town house, which is spoken of as being built by her rather than her husband, was regarded at the time of its building as a great piece of extravagance. I well remember it as I do also her country house, which was no less a departure from primitive simplicity. The former was burned in the great fire of 1846, and had not been changed externally from its original somewhat pretentious appearance. It stood on Centre

26

street, one house north of the corner of Pearl street, on what is now the lawn belonging to the late Charles B. Swain estate. A small front room was Aunt Keziah's shop. It had a bow window which remained to the last. My aged friend said she well remembered going to this shop with her mother in the time of the Revolutionary War, when the island was reduced to great pecuniary distress. Aunt Keziah, a stately woman, would take down the goods asked for, name the price—an exorbitant one which the purchaser would not or could not pay, —then without a word she would quietly place the goods on the shelf again, knowing that she held a monopoly and that the people must go without or come to her terms finally.

When a chamber of the house was being remodelled, some years before it was burned, a large closet was found that had no means of entrance except by removing a panel, which was so put in as to show no trace of its use as a door. The closet was undoubtedly used as a place of concealment for goods in the time of the war.

It was a pity to have the house go up in smoke and flames, and, with many other interests, be lost to the knowledge of the present generation. Keziah's out of town house, or, as it might be called, country seat, was equally imposing. It stood near the south shore of Polpis harbor, in what was known as the Simeon Macy farm, owned now, I think, by William Starbuck. It was larger than most farm houses, with the full complement of large windows, and, standing on a commanding eminence, was a prominent object in the landscape.

My aged friend was, when a child, at this house, and related an incident which is confirmatory of a legend alluded to in "Miriam Coffin," which says, "There was a subterranean passage from a clump of bushes on the shore of the harbor to the cellar of the house, designed for smuggling in goods from small sloops which might be seen at nightfall running up towards Polpis harbor." The narrator was playing on the beach with other little girls when they discovered in some bushes what they took to be a large drain leading from the house. It evidently had not been used for that purpose, and was high enough for them to stand up in. They went as far as they dared, and when they returned to the house they asked their stately hostess what it was. She gave them some evasive reply and forbade their going to the place again. This, doubtless, was the foundation of the author's legend, in which Peleg Folger, a brother of the heroine, is spoken of as making the same discovery as the children, and was effectively silenced from asking questions by his shrewd sister.

By Keziah's great business talent and political management she was enabled to obtain almost a monopoly of most of the necessaries of life, which were difficult of attainment on the island. During the war, when the people had spent their money, she took mortgages on their real estate. An old citizen told me that at the close of the war she held mortgages on a large amount of the island property. These she needed to realize upon in order to meet her liabilities abroad, and estate after estate had to be sold at auction. The purchasers were the persons or their sympathizers, who felt she had been an oppressor. The property was knocked off at ruinously low prices. "She stood it longer," said my informant, "than any man ever would, but finally had to succumb. I saw her," he said, "brought out of the house, which she built and would not yield possession of, sitting in her arm chair, looking dignified and stately as ever. She sat awhile, then calmly rose and went around into the yard. After this, live on the island in poverty, amidst her kinspeople and the scenes of her former greatness, she would not. Live a subject of the American Republic she would not; and, turning her back on it all, she went to the British Dominions, where she spent nearly the rest of her life, returning in old age to Nantucket, at the earnest persuasion of her only daughter.

The ruling passion strong in death, she attempted, but in vain, to recover some of her former possessions. After returning from court at noon, her lawyer called and told her it was of no use for her to contend with the law longer, to which she replied, 'I want thee to keep this in court as long as I live.' Preparing to go to the afternoon session, she tripped and fell to the bottom of the stairs breaking her neck, thus ending a strangely checkered life. She was a woman of much ability and great capacity for business, but, while inheriting the birthright of the Quakers of the island, their language and customs, she was wanting in their straightforward devotion to principle, which for over a century formed the island's real wealth more than its ships or its merchandise. "

Another character worthy of mention was Aunt Katie Folger, who was a great admirer of Robert Thomas' Farmer's Almanac, which she regarded as authority. Some of her grandchildren, looking over the almanac one day, came across, in the columns of remarkable events, the hanging of Quakers in Boston. Having always lived on Nantucket, where Quakers were so numerous and influential, this greatly surprised them and they exclaimed, "Grandmother, did they ever hang Quakers?" She was a Presbyterian, as in that day they were called, and to give her reply the more point she was reading from the Bible. Raising her glasses to her forehead, she replied, "Yes, children, they did hang Quakers and richly they deserved it."

There came one spring a severe snow storm, so late as to be remarkable. These same children, wishing to test the correctness of their grandmother's confidence in her favorite almanac, looked to see if mention were made of the storm. To their joy there was not. They went to her in triumph to tell of the deficiency. She heard them calmly, and said, "Children, Robert Thomas knew all about it, but it was too dubious to mention."

Cousin Elizabeth Black, as she was familiarly called, was quite a celebrity. She was chiefly noted for a stilted style of talking, even in the most common conversation. In keeping with Friends' testimony against all music, she could not keep even the jew's-harp, common fifty years ago, for sale in her little shop. I used to delight to stop in as I passed to and from school, and ask for one to hear her reply. "Cousin Elizabeth, has thee any jew's-harps?" "No, child, and no other harp that the Israelites used for diversion or devotion." An inmate of the house stepped into her room and asked familiarly, "Cousin Elizabeth, has thee seen my scissors?" "No, Abigail, and I should not be willing to go before a magistrate under a solemnity and affirm that thee was ever the owner of a pair of scissors."

Being quite a distance from home one day, she stepped into the house of a relative and said, "I am somewhat weary, cousin; will thee favor me with the use of thy horse and cart to convey me to my domicile? And thee must send a charioteer who will drive steadily."

She sent at one time for a prominent man of the town to say to him, "I want to solicit thee to cast thy vote and use thy influence to procure for my cousin, Peleg Folger, the office of Town Clerk. He wants the office not so much for pecuniary emolument, as from a thirst to reach the records and write a history of the island."

The most elaborate specimen of her style, which I remember, is her speaking to two young women who were her roommates while travelling, and who were disposed to talk after retiring. "Now girls, the time for sleep has fully arrived, and it is my desire that silence may pervade the apartment until Sol again ascends the heavens, unless some emergency should call for articulation." The quaint historian and chronicler of the period, Franklin Folger, thought he would put her use of uncommon words to the test, and sent to her little shop a note asking for a pound of saccharine commodity. This puzzled Cousin Elizabeth, and she had to resort to the dictionary to learn that he wanted a pound of sugar.

In 1825, Governor Lincoln was visiting a gentleman on the island who took him to see our friend. "Can it be possible," she said, "that thou art the Governor of Massachusetts, that I now see standing before me with my own eyes? Do walk in and take a chair. Thou art the first governor in the official capacity that has visited here since 1763, and the pleasure which I now take in beholding thee shall be written on the tablets of my heart till time with me shall be no more."

A friend called in a day or two after the Governor's call and remarked, "So thee has had a call from the Governor." She answered promptly, "Yes, I have, and it is beyond my expectations and excites my admiration that the Governor of the nation should come to visit me in my humble habitation."

I have spoken only of their quaint traits and speech, in a humorous strain. Do not take these as representatives of Nantucket. No place of the period contained a larger percentage of women who would be spoken of in another way—shrewd, capable, noble in all life's walks, domestic, social, religious. The circumstances of the place, its business and the large prevalence of the ideas of Quakerism put the women in a conspicuous place, a century in advance of the movements of our time in regard to woman's true position and sphere. Nantucket, with its Quaker influence, settled the question better than legislature can.

Sojourner Truth forcibly said, "If women want their rights, let them take them," and on Nantucket they did, without profession, and almost without knowing it. As we have said, with the fathers at sea the mothers were the heads of the homes, and homes that well deserved the name. They were a conscientious class, sending out in turn as noble successors as any place has given to the world.

Very early, there was the daughter of Tristram Coffin, Mary Starbuck, the first preacher among Friends, called the "Great

Woman,'' from whom an influence has descended which has contributed ever since to the acknowledged superiority of Nantucket women. She was esteemed a sort of Deborah among the people, and nothing of note was done on the island without her. Many of her family became ministers also among Friends. Although she left on the island but few visible monuments of her greatness of character, almost nothing she wrote having been preserved, yet her invisible monuments have been so enduring that for all generations after her her name has been on the island like a household word, almost a household divinity. So true is it that the memory of the virtuous is precious and their names are held in everlasting remembrance.

From early times there were women preachers and elders, at whose feet might well sit many who in the day of larger opportunity are filling in the world an honored and worthy place. I remember an incident related of one of these which has always profoundly impressed me. She was a preacher amongst Friends, while her husband was an elder. Both were held in high esteem, but the wife knew what the world did not, that her husband later in life was no longer worthy of his position. She was so deeply exercised that a stern sense of duty compelled her to call the ministers and elders together, and open to them the matter which resulted in his disownment. This, as narrated by one who was familiar with the circumstances, and with the deeply tried woman, has always seemed to me a sublimely heroic act.

The most prominent preacher in the meeting of my boyhood was Mary Clisby, afterwards Mary Macy. She is worthy of mention not for eloquence of speech or grace of manner, but in their absence she had a weight of character spiritually combined with a remarkable insight, which made her a marked person. In her ministry of sixty years—she lived to be about ninety —she drew from the deepest springs of inspiration ; and in her public appearance was often led to unfold and minister to conditions of which she could know nothing outwardly, and even of whose presence at the meeting she could not be cognizant, owing to her being very near sighted. Among instances of this kind, some of which it were better to leave in the obscurity to which time has consigned them, was one I will mention. At one of the afternoon meetings, I saw a man come in and take his seat far back. I had never seen him in the meeting house before, but of his general character I had some knowledge. He was a man of good natural abilities, and might have made more of himself but for the love of intoxicating drink he could not, or did not, control. Soon after the meeting settled into silence, our friend arose with the words, "Look not thou upon the wine when it is red, when it giveth his color in the cup, when it moveth itself aright. At the last it biteth like a serpent, and stingeth like an adder." She could have had no knowledge of the presence of the visitor, but she gradually portrayed his condition, spoke of natural abilities which had been clouded by intemperate habits, and then in forcible, loving language exhorted to amendment of life, for which divine assistance, if sincerely sought, was always to be found. This incident with similar ones has often, in the atmosphere of speculative doubts, taken a place as suggestive that the world in which we live is deeper and wider than we can know by mere outward sight.

There is Lucretia Mott, widely known, who became early in her life a minister in the Society of Friends, and who, from her natural breadth of thought, could not help uniting with the Hicksite division of Unitarian tendency in the great separation of 1828. In the anti-slavery struggle she took, with her devoted husband, a prominent place by the side of William Lloyd Garrison, Wendell Phillips, and the other heroes and almost martyrs of that cause. By her firm and consistent support in private life of the principles of the early abolitionists, and her testimony quietly borne against all distinction of color, nationality, and mere wealth, and by her persuasive eloquence in public, she exerted, through a life extended to nearly ninety years, a powerful influence for all that was noblest and best. If one wants to gather inspiration for noble, practical Christian living, let him read the lives of James and Lucretia Mott, written by their grand-daughter, Anna Davis Hallowell. The house where her childhood was passed until she was twelve years of age, when her family moved to Boston, is still standing, well preserved, at the corner of Fair and School streets.

Closely associated with Lucretia Mott was Eliza Barney, one of the noblest women of the island, or of any other place or time.

I might mention Maria Mitchell, of astronomical fame, Anna Gardner, another of the world's workers held in much esteem, Phœbe Ann Hanaford and Louise Baker as preachers, with a long list of teachers of unsurpassed excellence, ending with as large a proportion of noted housekeepers and home makers as probably any place ever furnished.

35

Chapter IV

T is now time we turned to men of th[e]
had a long list of as noble seamen a[s]
ocean. Wherever its men have gon[e] ... whatever walk of life, they have been the type that
makes honesty, probity and uprightness more easily
believed in. I once was introduced to a lawyer living near Boston, who was a genealogist and antiquarian. "What," said he,
"born on Nantucket, of Quaker ancestors, and trained in the
Quaker society? I will insure on that stock."

Like all seaport towns, the island has produced its full proportion of quaint men as well as women ; men who have been
noted for their capacity for story telling, and could narrate the
most improbable tales of sea or land, drawing heavily on their
imaginations when needful. Of very early date there was Jethro
Starbuck, the son of Tristram and Mary. He was not in the
least like one of the characters I have alluded to, but was a substantial elder among Friends. There is told of him an incident
which I like to mention. When he was about ninety he said he
had lived long enough and took to his bed. Lying there one summer afternoon, there came in a young woman and said, "Cousin
Jethro, we have lost our fire. Will thee give me a coal?" "Yes,
but thee has nothing to carry it in." She stepped to the hearth,
put some cold ashes in the hollow of her hand, picked up a live
coal, put it upon the ashes, covering it with more, and putting
her hand over it, started for home. "There," said Cousin Jethro,
"I find there is something yet to be learned," and rising from
his bed he lived some years longer.

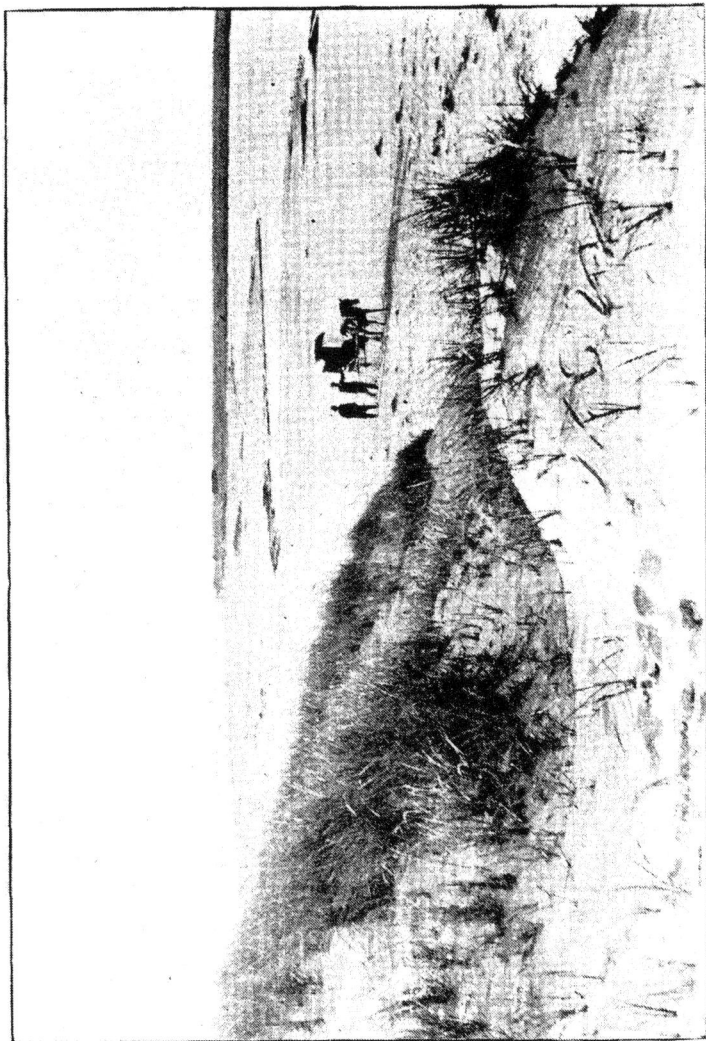

HUMMOCK POND

I remember hearing an incident of a very different person. When the first bank at Nantucket was started, some one gave him a check in payment of a small sum, telling him that it was the same as money. He took it home, looked it over, discussed it with his family, could not understand it and finally said: "It is a chuck; it is deviltry. I want nothing to do with it," and threw it into the fire.

I had a great uncle who was noted for great absent mindedness, which often produced laughable results. Going out one morning, he was overtaken by one of his neighbors to whom he said, "It is going to rain today and thee has forgotten to take thy overcoat." "Well," returned the neighbor, "I would advise thee to go back and get thy hat."

At one time his pig got out of the pen into the yard. He ran to a candle house near by and asked a man to come and stand at the gate while he got the pig back. On getting there the man said, "Why, Cousin Reuben, why don't thee shut the gate?" "Why, I never thought of it." Of the same man it was told that driving into his barn with hay, he was knocked off three times in succession before he remembered to get down in season. He had a brother called Uncle Ell, whom we boys of the family liked to meet, he was such good company. In 1799 two barns burned in what was then called the North Shore. It was at midnight in the winter; they were set on fire by lightning. There had been a prophecy that the world was coming to an end about this time, and when the people were awakened by the great glare of red light in the west, reflected on the black clouds in the east, many were much alarmed. One woman hastening by Uncle Ell, said in an excited tone, "Oh Uncle Ell, is this the last day?" "Why, you fool, did you ever know the last day to come in the night?"

Of the big story tellers to which I have referred, we had one who might be called the champion story teller. It was difficult to outdo him. At one of the islands of the Pacific which our ships frequented, there was a remarkable tree of which I used to hear our seamen speak. It was blown down in a severe gale, but not being uprooted had continued to grow along the ground. Its great length made it an object of curiosity. Our story teller was asked if he had ever seen it and how long it was. "Yes, I have; when I was in the ship some of us started to find its length. We walked about two hours from its root, when we met some natives who told us it was about three leagues farther.

When the firm of Hadwin and Barney were building their candle house, after the fire, the masons had used the ends of timber lying about to block up the large try kettle while they built the brick work around it. The blocking was so solid and green that after a kettle of oil had been boiled the blockings remained. This being noticed as quite remarkable, some one proposed calling our story teller to see what he would say. He looked a moment. "Oh, that is not much. When I was out in the ship, we tried out a whole fare of oil, and when we had done a hen and chickens walked out from underneath unharmed." A great laugh went round, and our friend's reputation remained undimmed.

Among the many anecdotes that used to be told representing the conflict in the minds of some between the Quaker principles and the usual impulses of human nature, is this. One

38

of the coasters in the War of 1812, when crossing Vineyard Sound sighted a small British privateer, and the crew saw a possibility of their being taken. The mate said, "Don't let us give up without some show of fight. There is an old swivel in the hold; let us get that up and fire it off." The captain answered, "Thee knows, mate, my principles won't allow me to take any part in fighting." "Well, Captain, you just go below and give up the deck to me." This he did, but could not give up the desire to keep the run of affairs, and just before the time for fighting he put his head out of the gangway and said, "Mate, if thee means to do execution with that swivel, I would advise thee to lower the muzzle a little."

Of solid as well as quaint characters, the island has had a large percentage. We can almost claim an inheritance in Benjamin Franklin, as his mother was born in the island, of Nantucket stock, and only went from it at the time of her marriage. The spot on which the house stood, and the spring of water which the family used, have recently been marked by the Historical Society. Dr. Franklin, as shown by his bust and portrait, has a striking resemblance to many of his Nantucket relatives. Christopher Hussey, one of the original purchasers, while never an actual resident (the family beginning with his son Stephen), was closely identified with its history and character. He was a man of marked influence in the earlier history of the colony, and was one of the crown's commissioners in setting off New Hampshire. In the early days of Nantucket his descendants filled a prominent place, especially in protecting the interests of the island in the war of the Revolution.

I cannot feel it quite right to omit making mention of the first Zacheus Macy, who, in the day that he lived, was one of the good doctors of the island. He was considered wealthy, and was of a benevolent disposition. It was said of him that whenever or wherever anything happened that needed surgical assistance or advice he freely lent his aid, and where there was need he was ready to assist in making the sufferers comfortable. When the Indians were being swept away by the dreadful plague, he daily, as long as it lasted, had one or two sheep killed and cooked as Indians did, in an oven of heated stones in the ground. These he would carry to a certain place and set a flag as a signal, while he kept to the windward and waited until he saw the food taken.

In the list of the noble men of the Island are the Rotches, father and son, Samuel Rodman, William Coffin, the postmaster, the father of William Coffin the teacher of Mrs. Cyrus Pierce, and the ancestor of several gifted descendants; Jacob Barker, who at upwards of ninety years had a counting room at New York and also New Orleans; Zenas and Gilbert Coffin, prominent Friends; Nathaniel Barney, William Mitchell, the teacher of precious memory; George B. Upton, an adopted son of the island, a man of great business energy and held in universal esteem; Barker Burnell, senior, much respected and honored by being sent as senator to general court; Peter F. Ewer, the chief projector of the enterprise of building the camels; Gideon Gardner, David Joy, and a host of others.

We must turn to the whaling service for perhaps our largest contribution. How well I remember in my youth some of these men, who in the roughness of sea life never lost the gentleman, or a certain dignity, which made them respected and honored wherever they went. Such were Captains Charles Gardner, Edmund, his brother, Paul West, Levi Starbuck, Reuben R. Bunker, Christopher Wyer, Robert Joy, Timothy Upton, Frederick Chase, Frederick Arthur, Thaddeus Coffin, Obed Fitch, Micajah Swain and many others whose names I have not space to give.

I want to quote here from our venerable historian, Obed Macy. "Captain Benjamin Worth has given us, by our request, the following statement of his adventures: 'I began to follow the sea in 1789, being then fifteen years of age, and continued till 1824. During this period, I was shipmaster twenty-nine years. From the time I commenced going to sea till I quitted the business, was at home only seven years. At the rate of four miles an hour whilst at sea, I have sailed more than 1,191,000 miles. I have visited more than forty islands in the Atlantic and Pacific Oceans, some of them many times, and traversed the west coasts of North and South America from Bolivia, latitude 40° south to 50° north, on the northwest coast, and up Christian Sound to Lynn Canal. I have assisted in obtaining 20,000 barrels of oil. During the last war I was taken by the English in the ship George and lost all I had on board. Whilst I commanded a vessel not one of my own crew was killed or even a limb broken, nor did any die of scurvy.'"

The following statement is from George Gardner: "I began to follow the sea at thirteen years of age, and continued in that service thirty-seven years. I was shipmate twenty-one years.

I performed three voyages to the coast of Brazil, twelve to the Pacific Ocean, three to Europe, and three to the West Indies. During thirty-seven years I was at home but four years and eight months. There were twenty-five thousand barrels of oil obtained by vessels which I sailed in. During my following the sea, from the best estimate I can make, I have travelled more than 1,000,000 miles. I was taken by the English in the late war and lost all the property I had with me. "

It was such men and women as these of whom we have spoken, an innumerable company who gave to the island its high standing, breathing as they did daily the atmosphere of the grand old ocean around them, strengthened by a business that constantly taxed and developed them, softened and elevated by the influence of a religion which Dr. Peabody of Cambridge said "was the best representation of pure primitive Christianity the world had ever known. " It was such men and women, with such surroundings from which the conditions arose, that led an English Quaker minister to say of the island in its earlier days, that the people lived so simply and uprightly that the lawyers who plead for money, the doctors who prescribed for money, and the ministers who preached for money found no employment. "The world goes spinning down the grooves of change. " Methods can never remain long the same, but must adapt themselves to advancing forms of civilization. The underlying principles and great truths of honest, upright, simple living are alike in all forms of society, forever binding and grand.

Here are some of the old Nantucket nautical phrases: "As much as to say salt marsh. " "Scudding under bare poles. "

"Two lamps burning and no ship at sea." "Going with all sail out." "Will come over the bar without camels." "Keep an eye to windward." "In the surf chock to the bow's thwart." Nantucket phrases ran through the island speech mostly without being perceived by the people themselves.

A woman sent a note to a carpenter : "I wish thee would come and put up my garden fence. My neighbor's hens get in, and my cucumbers are all made canoes of and my beans are under bare poles." A family circle was once discussing this use of nautical phrases, when the mother said, "Girls, I don't use them." "Yes thee does, mother." "Well, watch me and see if I do." The next morning she said to one of the children, "Take this and carry it to Cousin Phœbe, and tell her this squares the yards with us, and thee must scud for it is almost school time."

A Friend minister who removed from Nantucket to Hudson, New York, was once attending a meeting where the people were sitting very far back. They had been urged without avail to come forward, when he arose and said, "Friends, fleet forward, there is too much weight aft to sail well."

A company of ship captains from New Bedford and Nantucket were dining together, when it was proposed that each one give a sentiment or tell a story. One, in his turn, gave this :

"If navigating through this life
In poverty or riches,
You chance to meet a head beat sea
Just ease her where she pitches."

We must not forget to mention Abraham Quary ; not for anything in his personality, but because he was regarded as the last of the island Indians, despite doubt as to his pedigree of unmixed Indian blood. This distinction moie properly belongs to the daughter of Isaac Tashima, the last of the Indian chiefs, Dorcas Honarable, who lived in the Cartwright family, where she showed marked Indian traits. Abraham Quary, however, will go down to posterity with the claim of being the last Indian. He lived alone in a small hut near the shore of the harbor in Shimo. He cultivated what ground he could without question of ownership, procured fish and clams, and for the rest of his support depended upon kindly people in town.

Closely connected with Abraham is a legend or tradition of curious interest. When the great sickness of 1764, to which I have alluded, carried off the Indians, from some cause, perhaps from the action of some deep-lying law of the connection between all animal life, the blue fish, which had been plenty, suddenly disappeared from the waters around the island. The Indian sage said, "When the houses of the red men are laid low, the blue fish will return." Whether from mere coincidence or nature's law it was so. Not far from the time of Abraham's death, the blue fish reappeared. I distinctly remember hearing two men say that there had been taken at Maddequet, that afternoon, two blue fish, the first that, with possibly an occasional exception, had been taken for nearly three quarters of a century. Since, with varying seasons, they have always been more or less plenty.

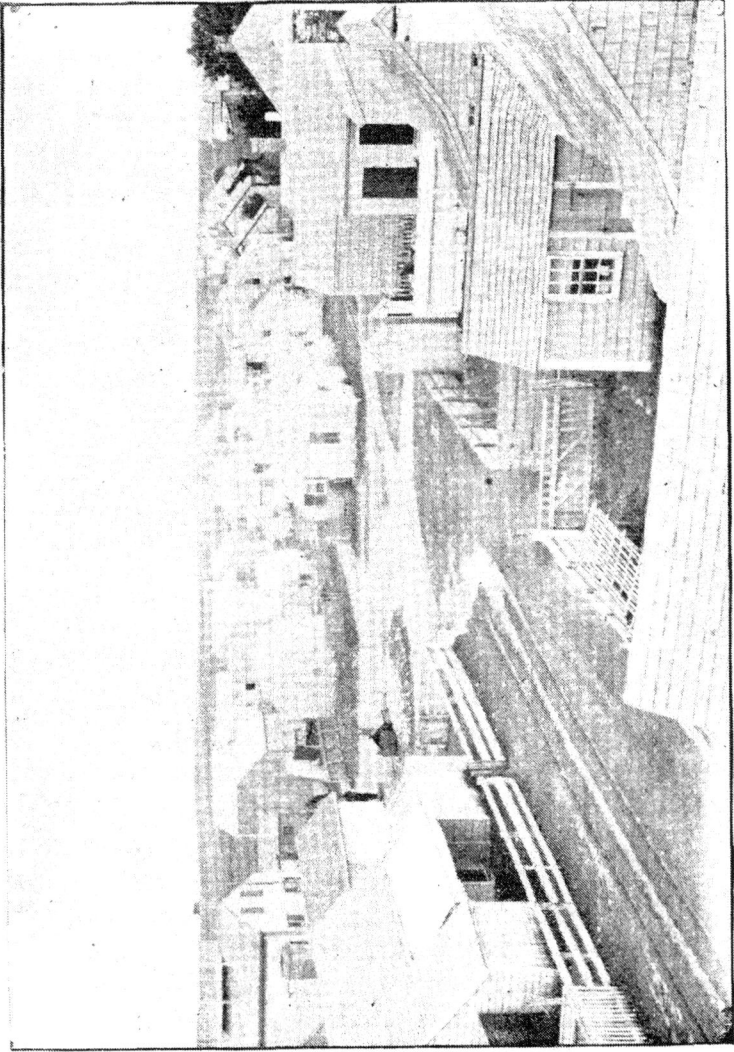

VIEW OF SCONSET

Chapter V

ET us take a visit to Sconset. Not the Sconset of today, with tall, showy cottages that look as if some glacier, of mistaken taste had borne them down from Cape Ann, but the queerest, most unpretentious quaintest little hamlet in the world. We start on a pleasant summer morning in the two-seated, cart-bodied wagon, pass through Newtown gate, a boundary that has become long since imaginary, and bear away southeast. Soon we are on the open plain, which Robert Collyer said reminded him of the Scottish moors, in the midst of fragrant bayberry bushes and sweet fern. We pass by on the right of the only farm house on the way, go through Madequecham's and Barnard's valleys to find ourselves in the southeast quarter, with Tom Never's Head looming up on the right out of Low Beach. As we ascend a slight elevation, the quaint village heaves suddenly in view, a long, low range of buildings with the glorious ocean for a background ; and on we go, down through the marshy ground at the foot of Cain's Hill, the air laden with the fragrant odor of swamp pinks, wild roses and blossoms of wild grape ; then another ascent and we are on the Bank. Winding through the little lanes, we stop at one of the cottages let for picnic parties, perhaps the William Paddock house, with part of the eaves actually lower than the rails of our wagon. It has for a tiny ell what was once the hut in Squam of the Indian, Isaac Tashima. We open the outside wooden shutters, sweep out the room, and spread upon the table such a repast as Nantucket women knew well how to prepare. A run

45

down the bank brings us back with voracious appetites. If the tide serves rightly, and we can supplement our meal with Aunt Sally Morey's fried fish tongues, all earthly wants are satisfied. Then the afternoon rest and stroll and we are homeward bound, perhaps through Squam, tired and happy. Yet with our happiness is a little regret. Our Sconset changes bit by bit. The heavy seas, hove in by the severe southeast gales, have made encroachments on the east of the island, especially at Sconset, the most exposed point. Rows of houses have been moved back. Occasionally a house has gone down the bank, and what was once the well of the village is now back of the breakers. Some one moved by the fact has said :

"O spare us our Sconset, old Neptune, we pray!"

We who loved the dear, quaint, old village, seeing signs of more lamentable changes than the encroachment of the sea could ever work, would echo the cry imploringly, "O spare us our Sconset, we pray!"

Another ride we must take, even more delightful, the ride to Shearing. Nantucket once had a flock of sheep divided at first into two parts, the eastern and the western. The western flock was given up before my day. A portion of the flock elected itself to the town, often to the annoyance of the people. Gates were no security against their entrance to back yards. You might stumble over them on the sidewalk, or they might choose to be folded on your front steps, if the steps were low, not easily taking hints to remove. The whole department of the sheep had much interest. The sheep ran at large, without shelter or feeding from the town. This condition seemed at first inhuman, but it was

46

proved that, take year by year with some off ones, these sheep did better and were freer from diseases native to the climate than those which were housed and fed.   Due to the humid atmosphere of the island, there were always green spots around the swamps upon which the sheep browsed.   In severe snow they huddled together for warmth, sometimes getting buried in the drifts.   After the storm the owners would turn out to rescue them, finding them by the breathing holes in the snow.   It sometimes happened that they were not found till they had eaten even the roots of the grass and the wool off one another.   Yet with it all they were hardy and the best paying property on the island. Late in the season, when the sheep were weakened, there would come what was known as the "sheep storms," northeast rain storms.   The sheep, huddled together, would drift toward the sea, and many would be drowned.

But let us go to the shearing, the gathering of the flock, and their owners, a patriarchal institution, like the sheep shearing of Israel, when "Laban went to Carmel to shear his flocks."   It was held on the second and third days (Monday and Tuesday) nearest the twentieth of June, on the banks of Miacomet Pond. The pond was used for the washing.   No old Nantucketer will ever lose the impress of shearing day in his boyhood.   If the meeting of the day before was a silent one, I doubt if any of us Quaker boys were able to think of much beside the morrow. In the night we would steal a look at the sky to read the signs of the weather.   If the day was fair no one needed a second calling.   Then came the start.   The horse and calash (cart) were backed up to the door.   First, the large chest, kept especially for this occasion, was put in with its contents—two huge pewter platters for roast lamb, a boiled ham, pewter plates and tumblers to match, the incomparable green currant and gooseberry pies, buns, etc. — and along with these the shearer's shears. Beside the chest was placed a keg of water and one of home-brewed beer. On top of the chest were put the old canvas sails for the awning and to shear upon. Then, with the small boys on top of the sails, my father to drive and the older boys to walk, with likely a shearer from the Cape, we were off, a happy crowd. As we ride over the Mill Hills, other carts similarly laden, vehicles, and pedestrians dot the level plain, all headed for the same point, about a mile and a half away. The day's business soon began.

The sheep were yarded in compact quarters, so as to be easily caught, and the owners picked out each one his own. Then, not soon enough for the boys, came dinner, most of the owners' families dining in their separate tents. And such a dinner! Delmonico's or the Parker House never came near it. Dinner was followed by more sheep catching. The sheep were now thinned out enough to give chance for clandestine rides on the backs of the veterans of the flock. Always were shouts of laughter ready to greet anyone knocked from his underpinnings by that " tarnal ram. "

A proposal, always met with favor, was to go outside the gates, where were flying horses, dancing boards, Cousin Eunice Noble and others selling buns and lemonade, candy and cigars, and blind Frank, the fiddler, making music — such as it was — for the dancers.

When the shadows grew long, we headed homeward, too tired to walk but obliged to, for the carts were now laden with wool. Next day was the same thing, and shearing was once more over. The heads of the tribe gathered to discuss the condition of their clippings as compared with last year and the market price of wool, while the children began to save their pennies for their next shearing.

The great island feast day was over. Silence fell on the deserted commons, and the tide of love and joy, of hope and despair, of life and death went on as in old times and new. Scenes change, customs die out, but human hearts remain a thousand years the same.

Chapter VI

THE æsthetic needs of our nature on the island have been ignored until within the latter half of the century.

The principle of moderation and simplicity had its root in a just estimate of life's true meaning and is pre-eminently Christian. With Friends it was, however, carried too far. Very few, if any, of the Friends' houses contained a particle of anything meant to minister to the love of the beautiful.

An amusing anecdote was told me of a personal application of this mistaken devotion to extreme simplicity, in the case of a valued saintly woman whom I well remember in my boyhood. She was so near sighted as to be dependent upon glasses. She had given her, to displace those she wore, a better looking pair, gold-bowed. Soon after she began to wear them, an overseer of the meeting called and, in the usual kindly manner, suggested that they were too worldly to be worn. The dear, conscientious woman went to meeting the next time without glasses. When the meeting was out, it was customary for the men to wait at the women's door for their wives. Our friend, with her imperfect vision, stepped up to a man, who in form and size resembled her husband, and took his arm. When she perceived her mistake she was greatly mortified, and on reaching home declared, "I shall never go to meeting again without glasses; if I am disowned I cannot help it."

Another case, more pathetic in its nature, shows the narrowness of Friends in still other ways. Years ago, there remained one other house on the site of the old town besides the solitary one which is still standing. It stood entirely alone, without fence or tree near, old and half decayed. There is attached to it a bit of homely romance that invested it with a certain interest to the Islanders. It was occupied by three maiden sisters in advanced years, when I knew them. Like many of that period, they held a birthright membership amongst Friends, and though ignorant, rustic to the last degree, and exceedingly peculiar, they had done nothing to forfeit their birthright and were supported by the meeting. The touch of romance is that their mother, who was of an old Friend's family, was, when young, sought in marriage by a young man whose affection she returned, and who was in every way suitable except that he did not belong to the meeting. On this ground her parents refused their consent. The young woman, as the story goes, disappointed, and careless of her future, said she would marry the first member of the meeting that came along, even if he was a simpleton. The first who came was almost that, but she kept her resolve, probably to bitterly repent of it in the long after years when she was slowly dragged down to his level.

At last the mother, who always kept some hold on the better life of her father's family, went wearily to her rest; and the three sisters, her daughters, who had become well known throughout the island, lived on, remote from the town, as uncultured and as much the children of nature as could consist with the respectability which their Quaker blood, dress and language never allowed them to entirely lose.

After they grew old and the house became unfit for occupancy, Friends were anxious to have them move to a more comfortable one nearer town. At length a house that would meet this condition came into possession of the meeting, and after great persuasion the sisters were moved into it. Their caretakers left them at night apparently comfortable in their new quarters. The next morning, going to see how they were getting on, they found to their astonishment that they had moved back to their old home in the night, carrying everything they could by hand. After this no further attempt was made to move them. Their invariable reply when spoken to on the subject was, "Why we was well enough off last winter, and we are only a year older now." Of the accumulation of years their simple logic took no account. So they lived on until one sister only was left. When she was taken to the meeting's home, the lonely old house was taken down for firewood, and the name of the family ceased on the island.

One circumstance in connection with these lonely women is worth mention, as a testimony to the beautiful delicacy of Friends in administering their charity. A flock of hens furnished all the sisters' means. They carried their eggs to the store of a Friend, who was instructed by the overseers of the meeting to furnish them with whatever their simple needs required, giving credit for the worth of the eggs, and charging the balance to the meeting, without letting them know anything of it. Thus they thought in their simplicity that the eggs paid for all they had, and a self respect was preserved which to even such as they was agreeable.

This little ditty concerning them may be interesting. The author is unknown.

On this little sandy island,
A mile or two from town,
Live three aged sisters,
The fame of whom resound.

One of these sisters, eighty-two,
Another most fourscore;
And Anne, youngest of the three,
Her years are seventy-four.

In peace and comfort there they live,
Free from the cares of wealth,
Enjoying more than many hearts
Of happiness and health.

No husband ever smiled on them
To cheer them on their course,
But a life of single blessedness
Seems to have been their choice.

They never left their native isle,
The world at large to see,
But seemed so well contented
In ignorance to be.

Full sixty years ago, they say,
They visited our wharves,
The price of apples to obtain,
Also of beef and pork.

They make companions of their hens
And nurse them with much care;
They share with them their humble home
And let them roost up stairs.

One of them walks sometimes to town,
In order to procure
Whatever articles they need
From Cousin Reuben's store.

Oh, it would please you very much
To see her in her walks,
* As round each post she three times goes,
And steps so quick and fast.

Gay visitors they sometimes have,
Also the sleek and prim,
With pockets well nigh bursting
With cakes and other things.

Could you but see the joyous smile
Around Friend Mary's mouth,
And hear the trembling accents,
As Phœbe then creaks forth.

" I'm obleeged to thee," Friend Phœbe cries,
And Anne looks her thanks,
While Mary hastens with the prize
As fast as she can tramp.

Upon the upper shelf she puts
The goods which they bestow,
And then she comes and seats herself
The news in town to know.

'Tis then the numerous questions
In quick succession come,
About the folks they know in town,
Also our friends at home.

*A habit she had

54

And sometimes, while you are sitting
Conversing with the three
About their hens and chickens,
You much amused would be.

Perchance your ears will be greeted
With cackling shrill and loud;
Sometimes a smart young chanticleer
Will make the walls resound.

And when we speak of leaving,
They press us hard to stay,
And make us promise often
To take a stroll that way.

"Now come agin, all on ye,"
Is Phœbe's constant cry,
As we, their mansion leaving,
Turn round to say good-bye.

Now if there's any in this isle
Who have never seen the three,
Delay no longer, visit them,
Repaid you will surely be.

The simple conservative clinging to tradition, illustrated by this case, as well as the disparagement of what was deemed ornamental, shown by the first anecdote, was evident in the education.

Nantucket's educational institutions, while in the main of great excellence, had their weak side, possibly from the isolation of the island or the nature of its business, but perhaps more because of the all pervading influence of Quakerism. It is probable that in Nantucket fewer persons have received classical or collegiate education than in any town in the State of corresponding size and wealth. This fact must not be taken for too much, however. It has been matched by a high standard of plain, solid, practical education, furnishing a sound business basis, and a large number of superior teachers who have supplied the town in the past and present, while many have gone to all parts of the country, everywhere a credit to the island and themselves. Nantucket has no need to strike her educational flag to any town.

Chapter VII

THE not infrequent wrecks around the island were a constant source of interest, at times sad and painful. When a boy I would lie nights in such storms as our coast knows, and hear the wind howling and feel it shake the house. Sometimes came a shudder at the sound of a signal gun from some vessel in distress. Then at "crack of dawn," as we used to say, our old seamen would be in the tower, sweeping the shore with their glasses for possible wrecks. At one time five wrecks were discovered at different points. Now horses and carts, with large numbers of boys and men on foot would make their way to the scene of the accident to save property, and not infrequently life.

How intense it all was! Once I remember nineteen drowned seamen were buried at the same time. Occasionally these wrecks left large sums of money on the island. In one case the amount reached between thirty and forty thousand dollars. The cargo, in this instance of cotton, had to be got on shore at deservedly large pay to the wreckers; then it had to be carted to town and shipped to the mainland.

The south shoal is a regular trap for trans-Atlantic vessels. It is thought that many never heard of came to harm upon it. The deepest interest was roused throughout the town one winter by an English steamer that anchored off Sconset, having consumed all her coal and every part of herself that could be cut down with safety. Coal had to be carted seven miles from town, then carried to the steamer in dories, that could be hauled over the ice or floated through the half-frozen water, till she had enough fuel to get her to the mainland.

Another singular incident is of a richly laden ship that struck on the south shoal just at night, with a heavy southeast storm coming on. The crew, seeing no chance to get her off, abandoned her, landed at Sconset, and the next day took the steamer for Boston. On arriving, what was their amazement to find their own ship already there. She had thumped over the shoals, been boarded by smackmen, and taken to port, a big prize.

When I first moved from the island, well I remember how tame life seemed without the exhilarating influence of the sea — its storms and calm ; its low tides and its high tides, sometimes sweeping over the wharves and up the lower streets ; its destruction and its life-giving energy and joy ; its majesty and grandeur, now roused to fury, now calm and placid, but never quite at rest ; and, pervading all, its deep undertone of soothing and of sadness.

MAIN STREET, NANTUCKET

C h a p t e r V I I I

S THE sea is to the inhabitants of the Netherlands a constant menace, so is fire to the inhabitants of Nantucket. A compact, wooden town, liable in winter to be cut off from the rest of the world, with high winds the usual accompaniment of the cold, the dread of fire was inborn, and the best of fire apparatus and all means of precaution were assiduously looked after. I shall never forget the nervous fear of those cold nights. Every now and then as a severe blast struck the house, some one would say "I hope everyone will be careful of his fires tonight."

The town for a long time was wonderfully exempt, a century and a half. In 1846, on a warm, moonlight night in July, the alarm bell struck, causing at first but little anxiety. Before the next morning a large part of the town, including all the business portion, had gone up in fire and smoke. Hundreds lost their all, and hastily left comfortable homes that night never again to own another. The town, already at its ebb tide, never recovered from the shock. Along with all the confusion and terror there were humorous incidents on that fearful night. A family by the name of Coffin, at a house early enveloped in smoke which soon burned, were hastily trying to save what of their effects they could, when Mrs. Coffin seized the package of silver she had put up, and rushing into the street asked a passing man if he would take care of it. He, not knowing her, said, "What shall I do with it?" Entirely bewildered, she could only reply,

59

"I don't know." "But who are you?" demanded the perplexed stranger. "Why, I don't know," answered the confused woman, "but I believe I am John S——'s wife," naming one of their friends to whose house their goods were being carried. It speaks well for both the stranger and for Nantucket that Mrs. Coffin received her silver—a considerable amount—intact the next day.

Some happenings of another nature are worth recalling. The house of David G. Hussey, a friend of mine, was soon in danger. I was helping to save something. We had his parlor carpet up, when command came to leave as the house was to be blown up. We did leave at once, and a keg of powder was placed ready for igniting. Just then the chief of the fire department, Obed B. Swain, said, "Wait, close the doors; I want to go over the house to be sure no one is in it. David is very hard of hearing." He was found in an attic chamber gathering up valuable papers. But for this thoughtfulness he would never have been seen again.

Later on, I was helping somewhere else to rescue household goods, with a horse and cart, when a relative met me and said, "Will thee come and take my mother away? Our home will burn soon." I went and backed the cart up to the house. My venerable aunt, Judith Hussey—then over eighty—had her chair brought and put into the cart. Then she came and sat down quietly, taking hold of the front rail. "Wait a minute," she said, and with a calm, serene look, but with indescribable sadness, she turned and gased on the house already on fire. It was a stately house, built by her husband and the home of all her married life. "Now thee may drive on," was all she said.

I started, selecting the least dangerous streets, but I was forced to pass over burning timbers, and to brush the sparks several times from my aunt's dress and bonnet, before we reached her son's. From there, too, as the fire spread, she had to be removed later.

One more rather curious incident I will speak of. Along the heads of the wharves was stored a large quantity of oil. As the heat caused the casks to burst, the oil ran out in large streams, some of it taking fire on the water. An engine had been placed a little way from the shore in the water for a better supply. A small island of burning oil came down upon it. The men, seeing the danger, dropped down under the oil and were unhurt, while the engine burned.

Many, on that fearful night, lost every thing. But there was a loss beyond dollars and cents that report would not be likely to reckon—the loss of historic dwellings; a loss that has grown with the increase of years, as objects of curiosity have been more sought by the summer visitor.

There was the house of the great heroine Miriam Coffin (Keziah her true name), on Center street. Opposite, on the corner of Center and Pearl streets, was a very fine specimen of the best colonial houses of the beginning of this century, a large house with brick ends, buttresses and fire chimneys, with a wide hall through the center and entered by stone steps with iron railings. When it was being built, a popular after-tea walk was to go to see the Tristram Hussey house. There was the magnificent mansion, as it then seemed, of Aaron Mitchell, on North Water street, the northern terminus of the fire, and the Mark

Coffin house on Federal street, one room of which, elaborately furnished, was used for a bank. Along with the rest burned the Athenæum, with its valuable contents, the Manufacturers' and Merchants' Bank, whose doors had just been closed, the Phœnix Bank and Insurance Office, a stately building on the corner of Main and Center streets, besides a large number of storehouses around the wharves, the repository of the accumulated outfits for the next voyage, or the returned implements of whaling to be overhauled for the next trip, along with many articles from foreign ports.

To an antiquarian resident on the island, and especially to a non-resident, these buildings would be now of great interest; for sentiment, while it makes no blade of grass grow and turns no factory spindle, has a place, and that no mean one, in life's great and diversified economy. "Man lives not by bread alone." After the fire had burned itself out, the scene of desolation was utterly indescribable. I remember one thing in particular. In the ravaged districts great heaps of coal and oily rubbish remained smouldering all summer. When the wind fanned the flames, they would shoot up and throw a weird, ghastly light through the streets. If the wind was east, the odor of burning substance would pervade the town with a gloomy, depressing effect.

At length, however, order was evoked out of the terrible chaos. Rebuilding began, new lines of streets were drawn, many narrow lanes almost impassable were obliterated, and business began to move. Encouragement was given by the sympathy and generosity exhibited in all parts of the country, made

62

manifest by large sums of money and household goods of every description. Nowadays, though an Islander treading the burnt districts sees only how much is gone, to the stranger the gaps are not visible. He is content with the present buildings which, although of less imposing proportions, are yet not uncomely.

C h a p t e r   I X

OMMUNITIES, like individuals, often win their lib-
erty and all advancement at a great price. Such
was the case with our American colonies in obtaining emancipation from British rule. No community,
I have often held, made a larger contribution to that
price than Nantucket; not, perhaps, by what was visibly done,
but by what was borne, and lost and suffered. With so extended
a sea coast, impossible to protect, and with the prevalence of the
Quaker principles against all war, offensive or defensive, a position of neutrality was the only feasible or indeed possible one.
This position was allowed during the war, and for the most part
was respected.

In the entire loss of business, in the difficulty of procuring
the necessities of life from the main land because of the nearness
of British privateers, in the untold misery of men taken at sea
and confined in prison ships, the inhabitants were subject to
great anxiety and privation. Obed Macy's history gives the following account of the economic conditions: "Many of the middle
class, at the commencement of the war, had some hundreds of
dollars by them which they had saved, but they were under the
necessity of using this for the support of their families. Wood
was frequently twenty dollars a cord, corn three dollars a bushel,
or more, flour thirty dollars a barrel, and other produce propor-
tionately dear." Have I not said truly that Nantucket, without
participating in active warfare, paid by its losses and sufferings
as large a price for American liberties as any part of the country?
No part deserves more the benefits won.

C h a p t e r   X

ELIGION is intertwined with the roots of our being, and lies at the foundation of all society; not theology, not ecclesiasticism, but the inward sense of a power above ourselves upon which we are dependent, whose will is our well-being and happiness, a sense of moral responsibility of trust and hope.

The religion of Nantucket has always been colored by peculiarity of situation and the strong influence of Quakerism. The North Meeting, as we used to call it (Presbyterian), the first religious organization, was loosely bound at first, and was soon overshadowed by the rapid growth, planted in favoring social soil, of the Society of Friends. It has, nevertheless, held on its way, including many of the most substantial people, and making a record among the progressive minds of the times by choosing as their pastor for years a woman, the late esteemed and beloved Louise Baker. The Methodists, Unitarians, Baptists, Episcopalians and Catholics have each in turn joined the ranks of religious workers. Each sect, not by creed or lack of one, but in proportion as it belongs to the church of the Divine service, by being the co-worker with God in human helpfulness, is putting its brick in the universal invisible church, the temple of light and love that the ages are building.

> " Our Friend, our Brother and our Lord,
>   What may thy service be?
> Nor name, nor form, nor ritual word,
>   But simply following Thee."

—Whittier

"God meets the throngs who pay their vows
In courts that hands have made,
And hears the worshipper who bows
Beneath the plantain shade."
                                    — *Harriet Martineau*

Whoever tells the story of the religious side of the island's life cannot but give a large place to the Society of Friends, its written and unwritten annals, filled with quaint, entertaining, solid and sublime experiences of human life in its multiform aspects. That its records* should ever have been taken from the island, where alone they belong, is a matter for deep regret. They should be returned, duplicated for greater security, and placed in some safe deposit for certain keeping.

Gone now its meeting houses, its people, its ways, but its influence lives and will never die. Its leading ideas and principles, based on the love of God and the brotherhood of men, its central thought the immanence of the Eternal Spirit in every soul, the accessibility of every soul to the Father, without the need of intervention of priest or outward form, these great thoughts are more and more pervading the minds of all denominations, and the divisions of sect and creed and form are fading out in the light of Christ's gospel of love.

The greatest cause for Nantucket's decline is undoubtedly the law of natural selection, the survival of the fittest.

The selection of a different railroad terminus has destroyed the prospects and depleted of its inhabitants many a western

*The records belonging to Nantucket quarterly meeting were taken to Lynn quarterly meeting after the decline of Nantucket meeting.

66

town; the change of a street crossing has lessened the value of many a block of buildings. New York, on the island of Manhattan at the mouth of the lordly Hudson, could not but become a metropolis and mart for many nations. Philadelphia, lying between the noble Delaware and the Schuylkill rivers, in a fertile region, the garden of Pennsylvania, must needs become great. So, Nantucket, with the sand bar across its harbor, with gas and electricity to take the place of oil, and with the advantage of maritime transit over land transit lost by the advent of steam, could but decline, and "she who once sat queen of the seas" must needs resign her crown of supremacy.

It was a hard-fought warfare, if vain, that her children waged to save her prestige. There were the camels, designed like those in Holland, to float her shipping over the shallow waters, that financially failed. The attempts at manufacturing and working of silk and straw failed also, because of the distance from a market. So the years went on of heroic endeavor and patient bearing, till her glory departed—yet not wholly lost, only changed. By her resources drawn from the sea she had given light to many people; by her resources drawn from the sea of its life-giving breezes, she still holds her place—not a mean one—among nature's beneficent forces. Here come professional men, merchants tired of the rush and whirl of life, exhausted teachers and shop girls, and sometimes those scarcely less weary with the inane life of fashionable watering places, to drink in restoration and a new sense of being.

Though many of her once stately buildings are owned by strangers, who occupy them but two months of the year, leav-

67

ing them closed and desolate the rest of the time, though her
wharves are crumbling in decay, yet is her work not done.
While the stranger, ever welcome within her borders, blesses
her, we sons of the soil, who too infrequently visit her, though
always hearing the note of sadness like the undertone of sea, yet
can say, now and forever,

"Undecked, unlovely as thou art,
A speck upon the world's great chart,
    Thou art our native spot.
And true to Nature still we love
And, by affection, still we prove
    Thy faults can be forgot."

———

" And yet that isle remaineth
    A refuge of the free,
As when true-hearted Macey
    Beheld it from the sea.

Free as the winds that winnow
    Her shrubless hills of sand,
Free as the waves that batter
    Along her yielding land.

Than hers at duty's summons,
    No loftier spirit stirs ;
Nor falls o'er human suffering
    A readier tear than hers.

God bless the sea-beat island !
    And grant forevermore
That Charity and Freedom dwell
    As now upon her shore."

Appendix

The following extracts are from a letter to the author, written by his valued friend, E. W. M. :

The history of one of Nantucket's most remarkable women. I copied it from an article written by Sarah Waterman, daughter of the Late Stephen Hussey. Sister to Eunice and Abial.

Rachel Bunker was taken ill on the 7th, Expired on the 9th, and was Interred on the 11th of the 11th Month, 1795, aged 80 years, 7 months, and 23 days.

She had 12 children, 100 and 22 Grandchildren, and 98 Great Grandchildren.

About 33 years of her life was devoted to Public Service. In which time she assisted at the birth of two thousand, nine hundred and ninety-four children, among whom were thirty-one pairs of twins.

The following lines were Inscribed to Capt. Reuben Chase by his Brother Capt. Joseph Chase, and were afterwards removed from the cemetery by his son Obed, who was absent on a voyage at the time of his father's death, and he being young, probably did not take the sense of them. Regret was expressed by other members of the family when it was too late to have matters corrected. Capt. Reuben had served as an officer with Paul Jones, in the Bon Homme, Richard, and seen a great deal of hard sea life, and Cooper in one of his Novels, calls him Long Tom Coffin. I think that can be found in Homeward Bound.

The Epitaph reads thus:

> Free from the storms, and gusts, of human life
> Free from the noise of passion, and of strife
> Here lies Reuben Chase, Buried,
> Who hath stood the sea
> Of ebbing life, and flowing misery.

He was no Dandy rigged, his prudent eye foresaw
And took a reef at fortune's quickest flaw,
He luffed, and bore away, to please mankind
Tho duty, urged him still to head the wind.

Rheumatic gusts, at length his masts destroyed.
Yet, jury health awhile he still enjoyed.

Laden with grief, and age, and shattered here
At length he struck, and grounded on his Bier,
Heaven took its Ballast, from its deepest hold
And left his body a wreck destitute of soul.

Nantucket, May 25th, 1822.

Ships, 80
Briggs, 6
Schooners, 16
Sloops, 59
Inhabitants, 7,266
Families, 1,423
Houses, 911
Rope Walks, 9
Candle Houses, 36

There were, at one period from 95 to 100 ships. I presume you may be well informed in all such matters, I corrected the omission of sloops, as you will perceive.

Nantucket, Dec. 28th, 1791, our harbor closed with Ice, and continued so that no vessel could leave our wharfs until the following March. British Letter of Marque was frozen in, during all that time. One of our first Ladies told me, she attended with many others, several very beautiful parties call'd Balls, given by the Officers of that ship, and they proved a very fine class of gentlemen.

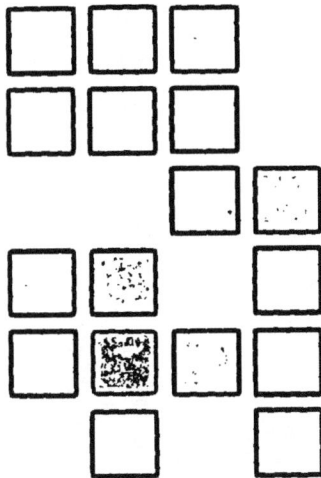

CPSIA information can be obtained
at www.ICGtesting.com
Printed in the USA
LVHW080502080721
692101LV00004B/78

9 781373 246493